Wives
after
God

Encouraging Each Other In Faith & Marriage

A 12-Week Group Study by

JENNIFER SMITH

Unveiled Wife

Wives After God

12-Week Group Study For Wives

Written By: Jennifer Smith
Formatted By: Aaron Smith
Cover Art By: Jane Johnson
Edited By: David T. Robbins

ISBN-13: 978-1490925387
ISBN-10: 1490925384

WivesAfterGod.com || UnveiledWife.com
Facebook.com/UnveiledWife
Pinterest.com/UnveiledWife
Twitter.com/UnveiledWife

Give feedback on the book at:
WivesAfterGod.com

Printed in U.S.A

*This group study is dedicated to the
people who have poured into my
life sharing the light of Christ and
teaching me the importance of
discipleship and to the wives who, all
those years ago, sat in my living room
and committed to seeking God with me.*

CONTENTS

Dear Wife,

It is such a wonderful blessing to share this group study with you. I desperately desired a resource that would encourage growth in my faith and growth in my relationships. I found just what I needed in my living room in the company of a few other wives willing to explore God's Word and what He says about marriage! The small group of wives I invited over each week helped me in great ways and I will forever be grateful for those precious moments we shared together. As God prepared my heart each week for our group time, He was using my need for community and discipleship to create this beautiful 12-Week study that you are about to experience. God had a much bigger plan with this study than I could ever have imagined. Taking it from a small group of women I know and putting it into the hands of many more all around the world. I hope and pray that this study is revolutionary in the two most important and intimate relationships in your life, your walk with God and your journey with your husband. I also hope that it helps you connect and build strong relationships with other wives, in real life. Be encouraged knowing that there are many more wives also experiencing the richness of this content, intentionally striving to be more holy as a child of God and as a wife. You are not alone in your struggles and you are not alone in your transformation of becoming the woman God wants you to be. Knowing that you are rallying with wives all across the world to make positive changes in your faith and in your relationships should be empowering! Thank you so much for taking the time to commit to this study, thank you for being a wife after God, and thank you for investing in your marriage. May faith, hope, and love abound, and may peace fill your heart!

Love,
Jennifer Smith

Dear Lord,

Thank you for this beautiful woman reading this right now. I pray a blessing over her life. May your Holy Spirit fill her heart with peace and joy. I pray that you would use this group study to help her build stronger relationships with you, with her husband, and with other wives. May you empower her as she strives to be the woman you created her to be. Give her the courage to share openly during every discussion and may you use the group time to encourage and teach her about your truth. I pray against the enemy and any schemes he may have to rob her of the benefits of experiencing this group study. I pray against any distractions that would attempt to keep her from attending each meeting or initiating the weekly challenges. Guard her heart and her mind in Christ Jesus. I pray right now that you would prepare her for what she is about to experience during the next 12 weeks. May you also protect her marriage from the attacks of the enemy. I pray her husband supports her and the time she is devoting to this study. Use this resource to make a powerful impact in their marriage. Thank you for her life, thank you for her relationship with her husband, and thank you for giving her the opportunity to join other wives in the process of discipleship. Bless this wife and continue to lavish her with your great love. In Jesus' name, AMEN!

PREFACE

Hi and welcome to Wives After God!

You are reading this right now because God loves you and He cares about your marriage. Whether you were invited by another wife or simply stumbled upon this group study by chance, the truth is that God is the one who is inviting you to participate in this incredible 12-Week study designed to help you grow into the woman He created you to be!

Wives After God was developed as a resource to help you walk alongside other women, rally together in the daily battles you face, and to learn more about God's ways. Most wives can relate with the natural ebb and flow in marriages, but how many wives have a place of support, comfort, and help, where the freedom to be vulnerable is abundant and God's redeeming love heals? This group study is designed to encourage and disciple wives in a positive environment, where wives can minister to other wives through prayer, fellowship, and accountability.

Discipleship is the process by which Christians are equipped by the Holy Spirit to overcome the pressures and trials of life and become more like Christ. This process requires you to examine your thoughts, words, and actions, while striving to make adjustments necessary to align them to the Word of God. Wives After God is a group study that guides you through this process, challenging you to examine your heart, with the love and support of other wives who are also eager to become more like Christ. Discipleship is important because as you become more like Christ, you become a living testimony of His great love story, spreading the good news of His message to others.

The benefit of experiencing a group setting is that you will quickly realize you are not alone in your struggles. Every wife encounters hardships, pain, and questions about life and marriage all the time. Participating in this group study will reveal the importance of connecting with other wives and the value of their support, accountability, and the wisdom collected from personal experiences. Sharing in a group format will help you gain understanding and insight as you press toward God together with two common goals: to blossom as a Christian woman and to better your relationships.

This study is designed to be shared in a small group setting. The directives are purposed for a wife who is willing to take a leap of faith and begin a group or to join one through invitation. This same study guide should be used by all participants in the group as they follow along with the leader.

The content in this group study was the inspiration for the 30-Day Devotional - Wife After God. It may be a great resource to read while going through this group study as it covers most of the session topics in greater depth. It is available at WifeAfterGod.com.

If you are leading a group please continue reading.

If you are a wife joining a group please wait to move on until your group gathers for the first meeting.

FOR THOSE PLANNING TO LEAD
A GROUP

<u>Here Is How To Get Started:</u>

Begin by praying. Ask God to help you develop
a list of 2-10 wives whom He desires to join your
study. The Holy Spirit is already at work in other
women's hearts, preparing them for this. Once the
names start to come, write them down, and continue
to pray for them, especially their marriages.

When you are ready, share with each wife how
God has placed this study on your heart and that
you felt led to invite them. It is very important to
stress the exclusivity of the group because it will
catch fire. Wives will ask you if they can bring a
friend, but you must pray about it before answering.
The exclusivity of the group fosters an intimate
environment where wives can easily build the trust
necessary for vulnerability and transparency. Be
gentle and kind when you respond to the wives in
your group; once they understand why the group is
exclusive, they will feel even more connected and
secure. Some wives may reject your invitation, this
is okay. Don't allow your feelings to be hurt! Not
everyone's schedule may match up and every heart
may not be ready.

You will need to dedicate about 1.5 - 2 hours per
week for your group time. Don't be afraid to take
more time if needed. This is when you and your

group of wives will meet and journey through this study together. Keep it on a consistent day and time - for example, Tuesday nights at 7pm - this way the wives know exactly when each meeting will be and can plan for it ahead of time. Deciding on a day and time may take creative organizing, but don't worry, surely you will find a perfect time to satisfy the majority.

You will ask each wife you invite to get their own copy of this study guide. That way they have access to all of the questions and challenges listed, as well as room to write down any notes throughout your time together.

Once you have the list of wives who will make up your group, the day and time when you will all meet up, and every wife has a copy of Wives After God - The Group Study, all you need is a start date!

Each session in this book is designed to be read aloud and discussed. There are 12 sessions in this study, which means your group should meet together for at least 12 weeks.

(There are a few other recommendations that may add a few weeks to complete if your group chooses to do so. Please refer to the end of this section for more details.)

At the beginning of every session there is a guided prayer that you may use to start off the session; however, you may pray your own prayer as well!

It is crucial to stress the importance of consistency in attendance. In order for each wife to receive the most out of this devotional, they will need to take responsibility for showing up, as well as completing any of the given assignments. If you make the effort to stress the importance of consistency and some of the wives still struggle to show up consistently, do not let it hinder you from leading the wives that do show up!

Your role in the group is to facilitate. You will be the one to read through each session and prompt the discussion questions. Even though you will be the facilitator you still have the responsibility to complete every given assignment and weekly challenge, as well as joining in any of the discussions. In addition, when scriptures are presented you should often delegate them out for the other wives to read to encourage participation. You will also be the one in constant communication with each wife, but you will want to encourage the women to build relationships with each other as well; hopefully, it will happen naturally. Sometimes conversations can get carried away into different topics; it is your responsibility as the facilitator to guide it back to the study material. However, it is also good to let the conversations progress, so use your personal judgment per discussion.

*Important to Note:

The wives in your group may look to you as an authority or as the leader in the group. If questions come up that you do not have an answer to, simply address the wives honestly, telling them you don't know the answer or that it is something you will have to research. **If you don't have an answer, it's okay. It's better to say that you don't know than to say something that contradicts God's word.**

If you want to read ahead to prepare yourself feel free! God is moving mightily using wives to share His passion for marriage all over the world. Thank you for being a willing servant to facilitate such a powerful discipleship group!

Also, at the end of the group, you will be encouraged to share a testimony about your experience as the leader. Please keep notes on your journey to help you prepare! Share both good moments and challenging ones.

Have fun and thank you for being willing to let God use you in such an extraordinary way!

*During the first meeting together with your group there is an assignment that each wife will need to participate in. Please be prepared by supplying paper and envelopes for each wife. You can make it simple or bring decorative stationery for them to use!

Additional meeting Ideas

These are supplements, not intended to replace any of the actual meetings.

Guest Wife Meeting:

Invite a guest wife from outside the group who would feel comfortable sharing their testimony and answering questions about it. Let the group know in advance so they can prepare questions if they would like. (This is a great way to expound on an area you and your wives would benefit from such as intimacy, finances, motherhood, etc. It is valuable to invite a guest speaker who has experience and can provide encouragement to your group.)

Date Night Meeting:

Together as a group, plan and prepare a special date night towards the end of the 12 weeks. Craft special invitations to give to the husbands. Use this as an opportunity to dress up and cook for all the husbands, honoring them. You can go even further and plan a special moment during dessert to say one nice thing about your husbands to affirm them in the presence of others.

Girls Night Out:

Have a girls night out where you all go to dinner or do something fun together.

INTRODUCTION

Leader:

This introduction should be shared during your first meeting together. From this point forward you can read out loud to the group straight from the text as they follow along.

Welcome to the very first meeting of Wives After God! We are here because God has pursued each one of us. God always initiates His relationship with us, giving us an opportunity to respond. Sitting here among this group is evidence of our response to Him. He wants our relationship with Him to grow alongside this group of wives. We have many differences, but our common denominator is wifehood and, during this study, we have the privilege of encouraging one another, advising one another and praying for one another. Let us hold each other accountable and pursue discipleship together!

This study is designed to walk us through an intense journey of experiencing God, specifically tailored to one of our most important ministry roles: being a wife! Here are some scriptures that support the purpose of this group study:

Please Read:

Colossians 3:16-17
James 4:8
Matthew 28:18-20
Luke 6:40

These four scriptures are foundational to the purpose of this group devotional. God has called each of us to draw close to Him, to know the message of Christ, to be encouraged, and to be a blessing to others. These things occur when we meditate on His Word and share our understanding with each other.

There are 12 sessions in this devotional, which means for at least the next 12 weeks you are committing to the following:

- Spending quality time with God daily through reading His Word, praying, and journaling.

- Actively engaging and participating in all of the given challenges within each session.

- Consistently attending every group meeting.

- Commiting to confidentiality and respect for others in the group.

Some of you may or may not be familiar with spending time with God on a daily basis. Whether you are experienced with this or not, here are a few quick tips on how to spend quality time with God:

- **First** you will need a Bible. It is written in Hebrews 4:12 that God's Word is living and active, so just as you would carry on a conversation with a close friend, God will converse with you through His Word. The material in this study is based on the NIV; however, reflecting on different translations can provide more understanding. Feel free to share different translations as you are going through scriptures.

- **Second** you will need a study guide to take notes in (some of you may want to also use a personal journal if you need more space to write). Writing is one of the most comprehensive ways to learn, because it forces you to slow down in your thinking process to allow your hand a chance to translate your thought. It is also very beneficial in that you will now have the opportunity to refer back to any archived entry and see your relational growth with God, along with any answered or unanswered prayers you may have written down.

Here is a journal entry excerpt for you to use as a guideline; however, there is freedom to customize your personal journal:

(Date) 11-24-10

(What God Is Teaching You)
I need to stop worrying and give all of my cares to God. I need to keep praying everyday. I need to lean on God's understanding and not my own.

(Answer Questions From Devotional)
My worry stems from fears or insecurities that I won't have enough to get by.

(Prayer)
God, please help me not to worry about my kids or my job. Please give me confidence in the plans you have for me. I pray that you bless my husband and give him patience today. May your will be done in my life. Amen!

When you spend quality time with God, growth in your relationship with Him is inevitable. The amount of time you spend with God and the length in words you write down are completely up to you. Just be sure to pray, read scripture, and record what you experience daily. If you have difficulty knowing what to read in the Bible, there will be guided verses listed at the end of each session for you to use as a reference. Remember, God wants to hear from you and He wants you to listen, the balance of both of these will result in great communication, the key to any thriving relationship.

Consistency is very crucial, both in your quality time with God and in your attendance each week for these meetings. Consistency reflects commitment, self-discipline, and trust. You are going to be building relationships with these wives and you will all be challenged in the same ways. This study will require you to take action! Some of the assignments will be more difficult than others; however, the result is a stronger relationship with God, with your husband, and with the other wives sitting next to you. You must understand that this discipleship process is only as effective as you are willing to commit, and the devotion you exert especially in your relationship with God, will overflow into your relationship with your husband.

Confidentiality is a must! Whether you know one another outside of the group or not, each of you has the responsibility to uphold the confidentiality of the group. Any intimate details shared within the privacy of this group should not be used to slander one's character in any way. Respect each other to the highest degree. However, if something is mentioned that is illegal or raises concern for the health of another, please voice it to the group and decide together how it should be handled.

Also, since this group study focuses on marriage there will be moments when you share about your husband. This is okay if done in a respectful way. Please do not slander your husband's character to the group in any way. If, during discussion, a wife bashes her husband, please stop the conversation and remind the ladies to uphold their husband's character in spite of their frustrations with his character.

The format of each weekly session will generally be similar, with slight variations depending on the topic. All of the questions listed in each session need to be read aloud, including any prompting to define a specific word. After first discussing definitions, you may want to use a dictionary to help aid in defining certain words to gain a better understanding. These questions are intentionally provoking in order to fuel the group discussions.

Please note that each question is unique, resulting in many different types and lengths of answers; some may even produce silence, which is okay. It may take some time to feel comfortable sharing answers aloud; however, the more transparent you are willing to be, putting aside any insecurities or fears, will result in great discussion, deeper understanding, and the unveiling of truths that God wants you to realize about yourself as a woman, a Christian, and a wife.

Others in the group may be fluent during discussions, which is good, but be aware of the sneaky tangent. Consistently chatting off topic can interrupt the effectiveness of the devotional material. Please be respectful to each other during discussions, especially to me (the group's facilitator) and respond to each other in love and gentleness.

By committing to these standards you will allow God to transform your life, your marriage and countless others who you will positively affect through living as an example of Wives After God!

*Sign below as proof to yourself and God of the commitment you are making.

_____

*Important to Note:

There may be questions that come up that I (the facilitator) may not have an answer to. In this event, I will simply tell the group that I don't know or that it is something I will have to research. It is okay if there isn't an answer or wise advice to every question; it is better to say that I don't have an answer than to unintentionally claim anything contrary to God's Word.

If, throughout the next 12 weeks, you glean wisdom about marriage from the study material and you feel it would benefit your husband, please share it with him. Explain what God is teaching you!

Additional Information:

There is an individual 30-Day Devotional based on the material in this group study called Wife After God which can be found at WifeAfterGod.com Please check it out for more awesome encouragement.

Please take a minute to post a picture of your group on Facebook, Twitter, or Instagram, include how many wives are in your group and tag @unveiledwife, #WifeAfterGod and #WivesAfterGod. This will let other wives in the community know who is going through the study, providing encouragement to them, and it will motivate others to want to start a group of their own!

The content in this study, although rooted in Biblical principles, are the expressed interpretations and opinions of Jennifer Smith. She is not a licensed professional.

There are certain situations in marriage that may need the assistance of professionals or authorities, such as abuse. Please do not hesitate to seek professional help.

Does anyone have any questions, concerns or comments?

Now that you know what is expected of you on a daily and weekly basis, let's jump into our first session.

Session 1:
Marriage By Design

Let's open this study with a prayer, inviting the Holy Spirit to lead each of us through this devotional with understanding and revelation.

Dear Lord,

Thank you for each wife in this group. Thank you for bringing us together. May your Holy Spirit prepare our hearts for this study. May you use this resource to draw us closer to you and closer to our husbands. Give us courage to discuss the questions and help us to be transparent with each other so that our experiences help each other in our roles as Christian women and wives.

In Jesus' name, amen.

<u>Assignment #1 – Love Letter To God</u>

Every wife will need one blank piece of paper.

On one side only, write a love letter to God.

Take about 5 minutes to express the desires of your heart; don't hold back, this is personal between you and Him. You can mention the condition of your marriage, your goals for what you desire your marriage to be, or perhaps any pressing prayer requests. Most importantly, at the end of your letter include what you expect to gain during the next 12 weeks.

When you are finished, place your letter to God in a self-addressed envelope, seal it, and put in a collective pile.

The Leader will be responsible for holding onto these letters; they will not be opened or tampered with. They will be handed back at the end of the 12 weeks.

Now spend about 2-4 minutes each giving a brief description of your personal testimony; including when you got married, why you got married and one thing you love about being married!

Ready. Set. GO!

Marriage By Design

What is God's purpose for marriage?
(Give the group time to answer aloud)

Please Read:
Genesis 1:27
Ephesians 5:22-33

Don't rush past these verses from Ephesians 5; they are the anthem to which husbands and wives should model their relationship.

God created the marital union between a man and a woman to mirror His image and to reflect the intimate relationship between Jesus and His followers, both of which bring glory to God.

Marriage is an opportunity to express unconditional, selfless, sacrificial love, just as Jesus did for us when He died and rose again.

Define Love
(After discussing among the group, you may also look-up the definition)

Define Respect
(After discussing among the group, you may also look-up the definition)

Although husbands and wives have needs of both love and respect, God intentionally chose to highlight the needs of love and respect because He created man and woman each with specific needs. He designed woman with a longing to be romantically loved and He gave man a desire to be respected. When the two are joined together they become one! He highlighted these needs accordingly in Ephesians to help us understand His design so that we can better meet those needs in marriage.

What are the differences between showing love and giving respect?

In what ways does your husband show you love?

In what ways does your husband show you respect?

In what ways do you show love to your husband?

In what ways do you show respect to your husband?

What makes it difficult for you to love your husband?

What makes it difficult for you to respect your husband?

The intimate relationship between a husband and wife was perfectly created and designed by God with purpose. Genesis chapter 2 explains that God placed Adam in the Garden of Eden, but quickly realized something.

Please Read:
Genesis 2:18

What is God's response to man's need for a helper? See verse 19.

God doesn't go straight to creating a woman; instead, he gives Adam the task of naming all the creatures. God created Adam so that He could share a love relationship with him. God wanted to give Adam an opportunity to participate in their love relationship. He did this by asking Adam to name all the animals; an important task that made Adam feel valuable.

Do you allow your husband and does your husband allow you to participate in your love relationship (marriage) through trusting each other with responsibilities? *(Give Examples)*

A love relationship requires trust. Just like God trusted Adam, husbands and wives need to have a foundation of trust.

What things keep you from building trust with your husband?

In what ways do you and your husband build trust in your marriage?

At the end of Genesis 2:20 it states that, "for Adam there was not found a helper suitable for him." (NIV) God knew Adam wasn't going to find a suitable helper; He used this situation to show Adam his need for one.

Do you think God continues to show man his need for a helper? If so, in what ways does God show man a need for a helper?

Please Read:

Genesis 2:21-22

Notice that God put Adam to sleep and then created woman. This means that man had nothing to do with woman's design! Women are God inspired, and when paired alongside man, they mirror God's image! God designed Adam with the purpose of marriage in mind, knowing that a husband and wife would mirror His image and reflect His love story, while experiencing for themselves an incredible and intimate love relationship.

Please Read:

Genesis 2:23-25

Adam receives Eve as a gift from God, recognizing her as his counterpart, not because of anything she did, but rather because he knew God and trusted God.

In what ways does God know you trust Him enough to receive your spouse as a gift?

Eve did not have to do anything to win her husband's acceptance and affection. She was received as a gift and she received her husband as a gift.

Do we understand that a love relationship is not based on performance? How does this challenge the way you view your marriage?

How is receiving our spouse as a gift from God demonstrated on a daily basis?

Your attitude towards your spouse, how you respond to your spouse, and meeting your spouse's needs before your own, will reveal whether you view them as a gift or not. If you do receive your husband as a gift from God, a gift of value, a gift of worthiness, then you would be motivated by God's great love for you to respect your husband, regardless of whether you think he deserves it.

Challenge:

Find a moment to tell your husband that you respect him and give him two reasons why. This will greatly affirm him. Then ask your husband to list 5 needs he has and strive to meet those needs throughout the week. Be a blessing to him.

This Week's Verses:

Acts 20:35
Ephesians 2:10
Galatians 6:9
Galatians 5:13-14
Matthew 20:28
Philippians 2:3-4

Prayer Requests:

Take a few minutes to write down any prayer requests and then close in prayer.

SESSION 2:
BE MADE HOLY

How was everyone's week?

Are there any answered prayers or praises?

How did your husband respond to the challenge from last week?

Let us open this study with a prayer, inviting the Holy Spirit to come and move through each wife's heart.

Dear Lord,

We invite you to meet with us and guide us through this material. Move in our hearts and help us to understand your Holy Word. May you transform us, make us Holy as you are Holy.

In Jesus' name, amen.

<u>Assignment #2 – Evaluate Your Priorities</u>

Take a minute to list 7 of the most significant priorities in your life, in order of importance (1 = most important).

1.

2.

3.

4.

5.

6.

7.

Be Made Holy

Sanctification is a key role in spiritual growth.

Please Read:
1 Thessalonians 5:23-24

Define Sanctification
(Give the group time to discuss)

Define Holy
(Give the group time to discuss)

Sanctification is an event and a process of transformation. Sanctification is a result of Salvation, believing and confessing that Jesus Christ is Lord and Savior, that He died for the sins of all and rose again on the third day. Through this belief and confession, followers of Christ are set apart from non-believers.

Take turns reading the following scriptures.

Please Read:
Hebrews 13:12
Hebrews 10:10
Hebrews 10:14
Romans 6:22
Romans 8:15

Jesus was sacrificed for our sanctification, so that we would be made Holy. So for those who believe, they are sanctified through Salvation in Christ. We are immediately set apart, adopted as children of God.

Although sanctification is the event of receiving Salvation, sanctification is also a continuous process of transformation.

Please Read:

Colossians 2:6
Galatians 5:17

Even though we are saved, we still have habits and characteristics that God needs to transform and renew. There is an inner struggle between our flesh and spirit; a battle to conquer sin and pursue holiness.

What types of things cause this inner struggle?

We live in a fallen world where sin abounds. Everyone is tempted by sin, but in different ways. Some struggle with addictions and idols, while others may harbor anger or jealousy. This struggle between flesh and spirit is a daily battle. The closer we draw to God and the more we allow Him to transform us, the more we will witness the process of sanctification in our lives.

What does the process of sanctification look like?

Once you have accepted Christ as Lord and Savior, God will send the Holy Spirit to dwell in your heart and show you areas of your life where you need to change and then He will walk you through that change.

Please Read:

Galatians 4:6

The process of sanctification may look a little different for everyone; however, there are a few key Biblical principles that we can intentionally pursue which will help us grow closer to God. The closer we draw near to God, the more in-tune we are to His Spirit, our faith will increase, we will encounter growth, and our character will transform to be more like Christ.

Here are four disciplines of sanctification that produce spiritual growth.

1. **Prayer:** Having an active prayer life means you are in constant communication with God.

   Please Read: Philippians 4:6-7, 1 Thessalonians 5:16-18

2. **Read The Bible:** The Bible is God's truth, a manual for Life. It is a tool used to develop knowledge, faith, and holiness.

   Please Read: John 17:17, Acts 20:32 , Hebrews 4:12

3. **Worship:** This is your love relationship with God. You should worship with a constant attitude of reverence, praise, and thankfulness toward God.

   Please Read: Psalm 99:9, John 4:24

4. **Yield To The Holy Spirit:** God's Spirit was sent to comfort us, to help us, to teach us, and to sanctify us. We are called to yield to His lead. When we sin and ignore the Holy Spirit, we break fellowship with Him.

   Please Read: Galatians 5:16, John 14:16-17, John 14:26 1 Thessalonians 5:19

Everyone's relationship with God and process of transformation is personal; but no matter what the differences are, the disciplines are the same and the end result is always to prevent sin and produce holiness. When we choose to pursue sanctification in our lives, positive growth occurs. However, the pursuit is not easy; it involves surrendering yourself. We must be willing to die to self, knowing that we will be transformed into something far greater.

Please Read:
Matthew 16:24-25
Galatians 2:20

Referring back to Lesson 1 and the mystery of marriage found in Ephesians 5:22-33, if Christ represents the husband and the Church represents the wife...what does sanctification look like in marriage?

Sanctification means we are set apart to be made holy, and we are made one as God's Spirit dwells within us. Likewise, marriage is an event where a husband and wife are set apart as they commit to a binding covenant and experience oneness.

In what ways are we sanctified or "set apart" as wives?

What changes occurred during the transformation from being a single woman to being a wife?

What transformations are you currently experiencing as a wife?

In addition to the four disciplines of sanctification, what are some disciplines for being a holy wife?

What is one way you can pursue oneness with your husband?

Challenge:

Go back to your list of 7 priorities. Next to your list rewrite the same 7 priorities in the order to which you currently devote most of your time and energy.

If spending time with God wasn't at all on your list, add it now.

* *If where you currently spend most of your time and energy is not listed as a priority write a note about it below your list.*

This week allow God to transform how you operate daily. Pray over your priorities and ask God to help you balance where you pour your time and energy. Be intentional about daily pursuing the four disciplines of sanctification. Also, take time to pursue oneness with your husband according to how you answered the last question in this session.

This Week's Verses:

2 Thessalonians 2:13
1 Thessalonians 4:3-4
Galatians 5:22-25
2 Corinthians 4:16-18
Romans 6:19
2 Timothy 2:21
1 Corinthians 6:9-11
1 Corinthians 6:19-20

Prayer Requests:

Take a few minutes to write down any prayer requests anyone may have and then lift them up in prayer.

SESSION 3:
A NOBLE WIFE
PART 1

How was everybody's week?

Did you make any adjustments last week to better focus on your priorities?

Let us open this study with a prayer, inviting the Holy Spirit to move mightily among the group and to reveal understanding of God's Word.

Dear Lord,

Thank you for the Unveiled Wife Ministry and the gift of this group study which has brought us together today. May your Holy Spirit use this study to guide us as we live out our roles as Christian women and wives. May you be glorified by our lives.

In Jesus' name, amen.

<u>Assignment #3 – Qualities of a Noble Wife</u>

Everyone take a few minutes to write down a list of qualities/characteristics that reflect a noble wife.

A Noble Wife

Let's each take turns reading a portion of this scripture out loud **Proverbs 31:10-31.**

Now that The Proverbs 31 Wife has been introduced it is time to dig a little deeper.

Go back through Proverbs 31:10-31, spending time on each verse, expanding on what quality is being revealed and how it is relevant for us as wives today. Throughout these scriptures are characteristics of a noble wife, see if you can find them all!

(Follow the example given below)

Read a verse and then open up discussion about that one verse using the given question:

Verse 10: "A wife of noble character who can find? She is worth far more than rubies." (NIV)

What qualities or characteristics are being revealed in this verse?

The characteristic in this verse revealing a noble wife is that she is worthy.

As qualities are being mentioned, take note of them, whether in your study guide, in your personal journal or in your Bible.

Please share other versions of scripture if available. Diversity of word choice will expand understanding. There are also additional discussion questions for each verse.

Read verse 10:
What qualities or characteristics are being revealed in this verse?

An excellent wife is rare and worthy. As women, we may struggle with recognizing our worthiness because insecurities blind us. We must acknowledge that we are worthy.

Do you recognize your worth or is it a struggle for you? Explain.

Read verse 11:
What qualities or characteristics are being revealed in this verse?

To be trustworthy by your husband is of great value. It shows his confidence in you.

What are some ways you show your husband you are trustworthy?

How do you know if your husband has confidence in you?

Read verse 12:
What qualities or characteristics are being revealed in this verse?

Intentionally bringing good to your husband is important. Make sure that everything you do as a wife results in goodness towards your husband and not evil or harm.

What are some examples of being good towards your husband and what are some examples of doing harm or evil?

In what ways do you bring good to your husband on a daily basis?

Read verse 13:
What qualities or characteristics are being revealed in this verse?

Searching and being aware of things that are needed for your family and working with a good attitude to fulfill those needs are characteristics of a noble wife.

Are you aware of your family's needs?

What motivates you to work for your family?
(Work can be an actual job or homemaking)

How is your attitude about the work you do?

Read verse 14:
What qualities or characteristics are being revealed in this verse?

"Merchant ships" are vessels that travel and trade for goods - taking extreme measures to provide. In doing so a noble wife brings a variety to the table, and not just the kitchen table! This means being aware of the needs of your husband and going above and beyond to fulfill them.

What are some examples of bringing variety to your husband, family, or home?

How do you add variety to your relationship with your husband?

How do you go above and beyond to fulfill your husband's needs?

Read verse 15:
What qualities or characteristics are being revealed in this verse?

It is important not to waste your day away. God designed men and women to have purpose and to DO!

Do you manage your time well or is it a struggle for you to organize how you spend your time?

Do you strive to be diligent with your day or would you say that you struggle with laziness?

In what ways do you spend time doing things for others, such as preparing meals for your husband?

What benefit is there to you for blessing others such as preparing meals, doing laundry, or other such tasks?

Read verse 16:
What qualities or characteristics are being revealed in this verse?

Be aware of your husband's needs and be diligent to fulfill them. A noble wife is not selfish. She is thrifty in how she manages to fulfill her family's needs.

What are some examples of not being selfish with what you have, but rather using what you have to benefit your marriage?

In what ways are you aware of your husband's needs and thrifty in how to fulfill them?

Read verse 17:
What qualities or characteristics are being revealed in this verse?

Be strong and work vigorously.

What are some different ways to be strong in a marriage?

What is one area you want to be stronger? Do you work vigorously? Explain why or why not.

Read verse 18:
What qualities or characteristics are being revealed in this verse?

Being aware of the good in your marriage is very important. So is being devoted. Remember reading the verse about waking up early and now this one mentions staying up late. It is obviously important to get adequate rest in order to be functional and diligent throughout the day, so could these verses represent the quality of devotion you have towards your husband and your family?

How often do you recognize the good in your marriage?

How do you show that you are devoted to your husband and willing to sacrifice your time to meet his needs?

What benefits are there to sacrificing your time to meet your husband's needs?

Read verse 19:
What qualities or characteristics are being revealed in this verse?

A distaff is a tool used for spinning wool and it is also defined as a woman's work domain. Diligently working is a noble quality.

If your husband was asked, "How does your wife feel about work?" What do you think he would he say?

Read verse 20:
What qualities or characteristics are being revealed in this verse?

Being aware of other's needs and trying to meet those needs are noble qualities.

Are you aware of other's needs?

Do you attempt to fulfill those needs?

This session is to be continued next week.

This Week's Verses:

Proverbs 31:10-31

Prayer Requests:

Take a few minutes to write down any prayer requests anyone may have and then lift them up in prayer.

Session 4:
A Noble Wife
Part 2

How was everybody's week?

Are there any praises we can celebrate?

Let us open this study with a prayer.

Dear Lord,

Thank you for today. Thank you for the gift of marriage and thank you for the gift of friendship. May you guide us through this session and may your words transform our hearts.

In Jesus' name, amen.

Read verse 21:
What qualities or characteristics are being revealed in this verse?

Being aware of how things will affect your marriage and your family will help you respond to those situations in righteousness. A noble wife has no fear, is prepared, and provides.

Are you aware of how things affect your marriage and your family?

What situations cause you to be fearful?

What can you do to respond to situations in a godly way?

Read verse 22:
What qualities or characteristics are being revealed in this verse?

Being crafty with the resources you already have and producing quality things will reflect the value you place on your marriage. Being presentable is important and reveals the value you place on yourself and how your husband views you.

How do you use what you have to bring quality to your marriage?

In what ways can you bring quality to the intimacy you share with your husband?

Why do you think being presentable reveals how you value yourself and your husband?

Read verse 23:
What qualities or characteristics are being revealed in this verse?

Your husband's character is important to your own character.

How do other people show respect to your husband?

Do elders respect him?

Is it important to you that your husband is respected? Why?

Read verse 24:
What qualities or characteristics are being revealed in this verse?

Knowing what you are capable of, being aware of your craft and working diligently are all qualities of a noble character.

What are you capable of? (In marriage, in your family, in your work, or other)

Are you working diligently in the areas you are capable?

Read verse 25:
What qualities or characteristics are being revealed in this verse?

Strength, dignity, not worrying and not fearing are also noble characteristics.

Do you see yourself having these characteristics?

If not, how can you attain these characteristics?

Read verse 26:
What qualities or characteristics are being revealed in this verse?

Being able to teach others or give sound advice based off Biblical principles reflect a noble character.

How can you be a wife of wisdom?

In what ways do you teach others or give advice based on personal knowledge or from Biblical principles?

Read verse 27:
What qualities or characteristics are being revealed in this verse?

Be aware of what needs to be done around your house and don't be lazy!

Are you aware of things that need to be done around your house?

What motivates you to do what needs to be done?

How will being lazy negatively affect your marriage?

Read verses 28, 29, 20 & 31:
What qualities or characteristics are being revealed in this verse?

Be aware of your worthiness!

Are you aware of your worthiness?
How can you live in confidence of your worthiness?

Do you place value on your life and on the work that you carry out daily?

Do others see you as worthy?

There are a few repeating characteristics throughout Proverbs 31 that defines a wife of noble character.

Discuss what you think these characteristics might be.

<u>Continued From Assignment #3</u>
<u>Write This List Of Eight Noble Characteristics:</u>

Worthy/Confident
Good
Works Diligently
Thrifty/Resourceful
Aware Of Needs/Provides
Wise
Trustworthy
Fearless

These are characteristics that Proverbs 31 is revealing. We need to focus on these characteristics daily and strive to implement them into our character, if they do not already exist. These noble characteristics will positively affect our marital relationships, as well as any other relationships we may have with family and friends.

Challenge:

Compare your list of qualities to the characteristics to those we found in Proverbs 31. Use this list to intentionally live this week exercising these 8 characteristics. Live as a noble wife!

This Week's Verses:

Proverbs 31:10-31

Prayer Requests:

Take a few minutes to write down any prayer requests anyone may have and then lift them up in prayer.

SESSION 5:
PERFECT POSTURE

Does anyone have any praises to share?

Let us open this study with a prayer and invite the Holy Spirit to come and give understanding to each wife.

Dear Lord,

You are so amazing. Thank you for using us to encourage each other. Holy Spirit, please meet with us and teach us what we need to know to have a stronger relationship with you and with our husbands.

In Jesus' name, amen.

<u>Assignment #5 – Posture</u>

Describe in four words your posture.

1.

2.

3.

4.

Perfect Posture

Define Posture

Posture is the position of one's body, and it can also be defined as attitude, the posture of the heart. Body language and attitude are very important ways in which we communicate to others. We use body language to communicate to God, our husbands, and every other person we interact with. Our posture physically reveals quite a bit of what we are experiencing emotionally, mentally, and spiritually.

Discuss different worship postures (prayer, praise, daily living, etc.)

Here are some examples of posture given in scripture:

Please read:
Romans 14:11
Psalm 95:6
Psalm 63:4
Psalm 123:1
Psalm 134:2

Why are these postures significant?

Below are some more examples of posture found in scripture that we can read out loud, along with questions to discuss: (With each story discuss the physical posture being illustrated as well as the attitudes being reflected)

Please read:

2 Samuel 6:14-15

What kind of posture did David have?

Please read:

2 Chronicles 20:17-18

What kind of posture did Jehoshaphat have?

Please read:

Matthew 26:6-13

What kind of posture did the woman have?

Please read:
Matthew 27:27-31

What kind of posture did the soldiers have?

What types of postures, either physically or in your attitude, do you typically have on a daily basis?

What other factors affect your attitude? Such as work or dieting?

What significance or meaning does posture/body language hold in your marriage? What leverage does it have?

What are examples of positive or negative postures for us as wives?

How is the posture of our heart, our attitude, exposed to our spouse?

Why do you think our posture is altered depending on who is in our presence? Such as other wives, family, friends, or coworkers?

Has your husband ever called you out on any positive or negative postures you have used to respond to him? If so, how did that make you feel and did it help you to be more aware of your attitude?

How is posture relevant to sex?

How does your attitude negatively affect sexual intimacy with your husband?

How would you describe Jesus' posture during His journey to the cross and while He was suffering on the cross?

Jesus exemplified perfect posture! How He responded shows us how we can respond in our love relationships.

How can we reflect Jesus' posture as a wife?

How will reflecting Jesus' posture benefit our marriage?

What positive changes can we make to show respect, love, loyalty and forgiveness to our spouse through posture?

Challenge:

Add four more words to Assignment #4, specifically pertaining to the posture of your heart, your attitude. This week commit to making positive changes in your posture, whether body language or attitude, and keep notes on how your changes affect your marriage.

This Week's Verses:

Romans 12:1-2

Prayer Requests:

Take a few minutes to write down any prayer requests anyone may have and then lift them up in prayer.

Session 6:
The Armor Of God

How did the challenge from last week result?

Let us open this study with a prayer and ask God to bless our time together and to communicate with each wife through His Holy Word.

Dear Lord,

Thank you for giving us the opportunity to meet together. May you bless our time together and may you guide our conversation. Please open our eyes and allow our hearts to experience revelation in our relationship with you, with our husbands, and with each other. Let your Holy Word saturate our souls.

In Jesus' name, amen.

Assignment #6 – Armor

List from memory the elements of the armor of God. If you cannot remember anything, leave your space blank; it is okay.

Armor Of God

Do you know where to locate the details explaining the armor of God in scripture?

The armor of God is incredibly significant. With the armor of God we are encouraged to protect and defend against the enemy and other threats in this world. To have a thriving marriage, it is vital that we are familiar with the armor of God and use it daily. The armor of God can be found in Ephesians 6:10-18.

In this passage of scripture we are reminded that the devil exists and he schemes actively. Verse 12 sheds light on the truth that there is more to this life than what we see. There is a battle raging for our soul and the souls of our loved ones. The following scriptures describe satan as the "ruler of this world" Ephesians 2:1-2, John 12:31, and 2 Corinthians 4:4.

Although satan is the ruler of this world, believers are rescued from his darkness.

Please read:
Colossians 1:13-14
John 10:10

As Christians we are promised eternal life with God! However, until that time comes we are living amongst the world, which means we live amongst the raging war. The good news is God has given us a way to protect ourselves and our family in the midst of this war. In Ephesians 6 we are given the armor of God to dress ourselves.

The question is: Are you putting on the armor of God daily?

Ephesians 6:13 starts off with a command, "Therefore PUT on the FULL armor of God." It doesn't say you are saved through grace and now you will always be automatically dressed in the armor of God! It tells YOU to put it on, and not just some of it, the FULL armor!

Let's take a look at what the FULL armor is: *(Remeber, after discussing definitions you may want to look them up in a dictionary.)*

<u>Belt Of Truth</u>

Define Truth

Do you rebuke satan's lies according to the truth found in God's Word? If not, what is one way you can start doing so?

In what ways do you surround yourself with God's truth?

As a wife do you have sincerity in action towards your husband? Explain.

How do you prove to your husband that you are truthful?

Please read:

Philippians 4:8

Breastplate Of Righteousness

Define Righteousness

Do you understand that Christ died for everyone's sins, forgiving everyone?

How do you strive to uphold the commands of your Heavenly Father and those given by His Son?

How do you love your husband and take care of him like you love yourself?

Please read:

Isaiah 43:25
Matthew 22:37-39

Gospel Of Peace

Define Peace

How can you always be ready to give an account of your faith? What condition does your heart need to be in to do so?

Do you grasp the good news of Christ's love story? If so, how would you describe it to someone in a few descriptive words?

How do you walk in peace, especially when you interact at home with your husband?

Would you say that you are a bearer of peace or of discord? Explain.

How often do you intentionally claim and strive for the gospel of peace, freedom and harmony within your marriage?

Please read:
1 Peter 3:15
2 Thessalonians 3:16

Shield Of Faith

Define Faith

Is your faith in God unwavering? Explain.

In what ways do you trust God?

Do you believe you can "extinguish all the flaming arrows of the evil one" including his schemes against marriage?

How often do you intentionally "extinguish all the flaming arrows of the evil one" that come against your marriage?

How does your faith help you extinguish all the flaming arrows or schemes of the enemy?

Please read:
Hebrews 11:1
1 Peter 1:3-9

Helmet Of Salvation

Define Salvation

Do you appreciate what Christ sacrificed
so that you may live with God in eternity?
Explain.

How do you feel about the extent to which He
suffered on your behalf?

Do you accept Christ as your personal Lord
and Savior, believing in your heart that He
died for you and rose again and do you confess
this with your mouth? What impact does
believing and confessing this have on your
marriage?

How do you feel towards those that are lost
and lonely, those who do not have a personal
relationship with Jesus?

How does marriage reflect God's love story, the
unconditional love and sacrifice of Christ?

Please read:

John 3:16
Romans 10:9
Isaiah 53:5
Ephesians 5:22-30

Sword Of The Spirit (Word Of God)

Define The Word Of God

In what ways do you live by the Word of God?

What scriptures do you know by heart to use as a weapon against the enemy, just as Jesus did in the desert?

How often do you meditate on God's Word to understand the foundation of your belief in Him?

Do you see the words in the Bible as alive, God's Holy Spirit teaching you His ways?

Do you speak the promises of the scriptures over your husband and family? If so, what verses do you use and how do you do it?

Please read:

John 1:1- 5
Matthew 4:4
Hebrews 4:12
2 Peter 1:3-4

<u>Pray In All Occasions</u>

Define Prayer

How can you pray in all occasions, good and bad?

What keeps you from praying without ceasing?

Do you communicate with God daily?

How often do you pray for your loved ones?

Do you take time to pray protection over your marriage and family? Explain.

When you pray, do you feel it is important to thank God with a humble heart? If so, why?

Please read:

James 5:13
James 5:16
1 Thessalonians 5:16-18
Colossians 4:2

The armor of God has been given to us by our God, our King; laid out before us as a tool to protect and defend! They are disciplines that we should be actively doing daily! God is calling His army, His body, His followers, to fight against the evil one!

Will you put on the full armor of God daily?

Challenge:

Go back to your list of what you wrote about the armor of God. Next to your list write each tool God gives us in Ephesians 6:10-18. Spend this week memorizing the armor of God, putting it on daily. Also, be aware of the enemy's flaming arrows against your marriage. If there are any, write them down and pray specifically for God to help you extinguish them. Pray protection over your family and specifically over your marriage daily!

This Week's Verses:

2 Corinthians 2:14-16,
2 Chronicles 14:11
1 John 5:3-5
1 Corinthians 15:51
1 Corinthians 15:57-58
1 Timothy 6:12-16

Prayer Requests:

Take a few minutes to write down any prayer requests anyone may have and then lift them up in prayer.

108

SESSION 7:
FEAR & WISDOM

Are there any praises or breakthroughs you experienced during the week?

What are some flaming arrows coming against your marriage that you prayed for last week?

Let us open this study with a prayer, inviting the Holy Spirit to come and move through each of our hearts.

Dear Lord,

Thank you for bringing all of us together tonight. We invite your Holy Spirit to join us, lead us, and teach us. May you soften our hearts and open our ears so that we may gain understanding. We pray that this session would help us become better women and better wives.

In Jesus' name, amen.

Assignment #7 – Do Not Be Afraid

Write down this verse somewhere you will see it everyday to encourage you not to be afraid.

"For I am the Lord your God who takes hold of your right hand and says to you, Do not fear; I will help you."

- Isaiah 41:13 (NIV)

Fear & Wisdom

Define Fear

Fear is a distressing emotion caused by the presence or imminence of danger, whether that danger is actual or perceived. Fear cripples our ability to live life as God intended us to. When fear is fed, our faith falters. Being afraid, worried, or even discouraged keeps us from experiencing extraordinary, especially in marriage.

What fears did you have regarding marriage before you became a wife?

What fears have you overcome since marriage?

What fears currently debilitate you emotionally, physically, mentally, or spiritually?

What is the ONLY thing you should fear?
GOD!

Please read:

2 Timothy 1:7

Fear is not a spirit from God.

In Judges 7:3, before God gives Midian into the hands of the Israelites He asks Gideon to downsize the army. Read the scripture and take a look to see who is separated first.

God separates first those that are scared.

Do you think God can effectively use people who operate in fear?

Please read:

Matthew 14: 22-31

The disciples in the boat were scared of the waves thrashing around them. When Jesus comes walking towards them, their fear switches from impending doom to thinking they were seeing a ghost. Their eyes were deceiving them. Then Peter, recognizing the figure as Jesus, walks out onto the water. Doubt fills Peter's heart and he falls beneath the waves. God was defying the laws of nature and making history; Peter was amidst a miracle and got scared out of it!

In what instances has God invited you to do something, but you were too scared to complete it?

Have your eyes ever deceived you, causing fear to stir in your hearts?

What if Jesus said aloud to you, "Why do you doubt?" How would you respond to Him?

In what ways has fear affected your relationship with your husband?

Has fear ever kept you from doing something with your husband?

Matthew 10:28 says to be afraid of the one who can take both your body and soul!

Please read:

Exodus 20:20
Deuteronomy 5:29

We are only supposed to fear God!

Please read:

Genesis 3:6

Eve desired wisdom, ate the fruit, and gave to her husband to eat. Her pursuit was wisdom. What Eve missed was that the key to wisdom is to fear God. If she feared God she would have been able to resist temptation and just ask the Lord for wisdom. As wives we need to fear God and ask Him for wisdom, instead of trying to do things our way.

What does it mean to fear God?

How is being scared and fearing God different?

Why do you think that fearing God is the beginning of wisdom?

Who feared God in the Bible? Give examples.

Please read:

Exodus 1:15-22
Acts 4:19-20

If you operate out fear of God how would you live differently, especially in your role as a wife?

God is powerful and He wants us to know how powerful He is. The Old Testament is packed full of awesome stories revealing God's power!

Please read:

Joshua 4:23-24

If we allow fear to control us we are saying, "God you are not mighty or powerful enough!" If we fear God we are saying, "God I trust you NO MATTER WHAT!"

Please read:

Job 1:8-12

Does Job fear God for nothing?

Do you fear God only because God has done things for you? Explain.

Why is it important to fear God at all times?

Does God have enough confidence in you that He would boast about you before the enemy?

We need to make sure we are not just fearing God in the good times or the easy times. The enemy is always trying to find a way in to get us to break our union with God. Our fear of God cannot come from things He has blessed us with or protected us from. We need to have the mentality, "NO MATTER WHAT!"

If we give power to insecurity, fear, anxiety, etc. we are saying, "God you are not big enough to cover these things." Then, we fall beneath the waves, just as Peter did. God does not want us to fear because it impairs our ability to live out extraordinary.

Challenge:

Face your fears with God-confidence. If there is something you feel God is calling you to do in your marriage, but fear has stopped you, do it this week! Perhaps it is a conversation, a confession, or an act of love that requires humility. Pray and ask God to guide you and give you confidence and wisdom.

This Week's Verses:

Job 28:28
Psalm 111:10
Proverbs 15:33
Isaiah 33:6
Genesis 3:6
Psalm 37:30
Proverbs 2:10
Proverbs 2:4-6
James 1:5

Prayer Requests:

Take a few minutes to write down any prayer requests anyone may have and then lift them up in prayer.

SESSION 8:
PRESSURES OF THE WORLD

How was everyone's week?

Are there any answered prayers or praises from the week?

Were you able to overcome any fears in your marriage this last week?

Let's open this study with a prayer, asking God to guide us through this session.

Dear Lord,

You are so amazing! We submit our lives to you and we surrender our hearts to you. May your Holy Spirit transform us into the women you created us to be. Please guide our discussion and may you be glorified.

In Jesus' name, amen.

<u>Assignment #8– Acknowledge Things That Pressure You</u>

Write a prayer to God, acknowledging the things in your life that burden you with pressure. Ask God to help you identify what those pressures are and then ask Him to set you free from them.

Pressures Of The World

What pressures do you face as a woman?

What pressures do you face as a wife?

What pressures do you face as a woman in the church?

Where do you find your confidence?

What does the Bible say about being a woman and a wife?

Instead of feeling pressured by society or even by our husbands, we need to understand who God calls us to be. If you are wondering how to figure out who God calls you to be, you need to dig into God's Word!

God doesn't call us to have a perfect body, BUT he does call us to treat our bodies as a temple of the Holy Spirit!

Please read:
1 Corinthians 6:12-20

God warns us that beauty is fleeting, encouraging us to reflect His character and to fear Him.

Please read:
Proverbs 31:30

God calls us to be wise.

Please read:
Proverbs 24:3-4

God calls us to be intimate with Him.

Please read:
James 4:8a

God calls us to be submissive.

Please read:
James 4:7

God calls us to be Holy.

Please read:
1 Peter 1:15-16

God calls us to be righteous.

Please read:
1 Timothy 6:11

God calls us to be loving.

Please read:
Matthew 22:37-40

God calls us to forgive others.

Please read:
Ephesians 4:32

There are plenty more characteristics God calls us to be. He desires us and gives us the tools to be virtuous women who uphold Biblical standards of truth. Before we allow society or even marriage to pressure us into being women, we need to fully know what God calls us to be, which is found throughout His Word. Love God's Word, meditate on it, memorize it, saturate your soul with it, and as you abide, God's character will manifest in you.

Please read:

Luke 1:5-25

Verse 25 mentions that Elizabeth walked in the burden of being barren, for in that culture and time period being barren was a disgrace. Elizabeth felt pressure from society.

What emotions do you think Elizabeth felt because she was barren?

Define Barren

One definition of barren is "without." In what ways do you feel barren or "without" in marriage? (This can mean actually barren or if there is another area of your marriage in which you feel lack or without.)

What emotions does feeling barren or without evoke in you?

Do you carry a weight or burden of disappointment towards your husband? Explain.

Why is it important to respond to your husband out of faith and not disappointment?

Elizabeth could have responded to her husband out of frustration for the pressure she felt to have children. Instead, she trusted God and He fulfilled that desire of hers. Be mindful of the pressures that may tempt you to react towards your husband out of frustration. Set an example for other women by striving to have a character like God!

Challenge:

Try to identify other pressures that may burden you, write them down and pray that God helps you to not let those things affect you or your marriage. If there are pressures that you receive from your husband, find time to communicate with him about how it makes you feel. Seek resolution.

*If you are up for an additional challenge, there are a group of wives in the world who face very difficult pressures and could use some encouragement. Please go to http://unveiledwife. com/celebrity-letters and choose a celebrity wife to encourage!

This Week's Verses:

John 1:1
1 John 4:8
Corinthians 13
John 13:34
Ephesians 5:1-2
Psalm 139

Prayer Requests:

Take a few minutes to write down any prayer requests anyone may have and then lift them up in prayer.

SESSION 9:
FERVENT PRAYER

Are there any answered prayers or praises from last week that we can celebrate?

Who did the extra challenge from last week and what were your thoughts about it?

Let us open this study with a prayer and invite the Holy Spirit to be present among us, preparing all of our hearts for this lesson.

Dear Lord,

Thank you for giving us the opportunity to meet together. May you join us, teach us, and transform us. Use each one of us to help each other through encouragement and prayer. May your will be done through us.

In Jesus' name, amen.

Assignment #9 – Prayer Requests

Take a few minutes to list any and all prayer requests you have. When you are finished wait patiently for the rest of your group before you continue.

<u>Assignment #9 – Prayer Requests</u>

<u>Assignment #9 – Prayer Requests</u>

Fervent Prayer

How would you describe your prayer life?

Why is it important to pray?

How would you describe your relationship with your husband?

How does your relationship with your husband affect your prayer life?

How often do you specifically pray for your husband and your marriage?

Please read:

Colossians 4:2
1 Thessalonians 5:16-18

What things can you thank God for when you pray?

Please read:

Hebrews 5:7

What things are you petitioning for regarding you marriage?

Please read:

James 5:13-16

What sins do you need to confess?
If you do not feel comfortable sharing here,
please talk to at least one person at another
time. And whenever someone confesses sins to
you, be sure to pray for them at that moment.

Please read:

1 Peter 3:11-12
Matthew 21:21-22

Do you truly believe when you pray or does doubt reside in your heart? Explain.

Please read:

Romans 12:11-13

Define Fervor/ Fervent

Please read:

Matthew 6:5-14
Matthew 26:40-42

Have you ever prayed as Jesus did, wanting to not do something, especially in marriage? Explain.

Ultimately, did you pray for God's will to be done, or your own?

Please read:

Matthew 19:13

Mark 10:16

Have you ever placed your hands on your husband to pray over him and bless him?

What things would keep you from laying hands on your husband to pray for him?

Please read:

Matthew 18:20

Right now, with your prayer requests in front of you, take turns laying your hands on each other, praying over each other using the lists you made. Every wife should take a turn to pray over the wife being prayed for. Do this one person at a time.

Challenge:

Pray fervently every day, especially lifting up your husband and your marriage. Take time this week to place your hands on your husband, pray over him and bless him. You can also ask your husband if there is anything specific he needs prayer for and then pray together.

*If your husband rejects your invitation to pray, you may feel very hurt, but do not lose your fervor. Do as Jesus commands in Matthew 6, go into your room and pray for your husband. Believe in faith that God will soften his heart and that he will pray with you one day soon.

This Week's Verses:

Psalm 107:28-30
Matthew 7:7
Mark 9:29
John 14:13-14
Ephesians 6:18
Romans 8:26

Prayer Requests:

Take a few minutes to write down any prayer requests anyone may have and then lift them up in prayer.

Session 10:
Gifts & Fruits Of The Spirit

How was everyone's week?

Did God reveal anything spectacular to you?

Let us open this study with a prayer.

Dear Lord,

Thank you so much for each wife who is here. May your Holy Spirit lead us through this session and may you anoint us with understanding. Please reveal areas in our lives where we need to make adjustments and changes so that we glorify you.

In Jesus' name, amen.

Assignment #10 – Evaluating Strengths and Weakness

Take about 5 minutes to list your strengths in life. Anything that you feel you are good at, including talents, skills, characteristics, and insights. Also, note any weaknesses that you have.

Gifts & Fruits Of The Spirit

Here are some encouraging verses regardless of your strengths or weaknesses.

Please read:
Philippians 4:13
Isaiah 40:29
2 Corinthians 12:9-10

Let us first dive into the Gifts Of The Spirit:

One of the greatest gifts God has given to us is the gift of the Holy Spirit.

Who is the Holy Spirit?

The Holy Spirit is God's Spirit. When Jesus left Earth, the Holy Spirit was sent to us to dwell within believers, to teach us and remind us of all that Jesus had said.

Please read:
1 Corinthians 2:10-11
John 14:15-17
John 14:25-27

What are the Gifts of the Spirit?

Paul mentions the gifts of the Spirit in 1 Corinthians 12:1-11 **(Please read)**

What is there a variety of?

What is constant or the same?

Why are the gifts given to people?

What are the gifts listed in 1 Corinthians 12:1-11?

There are additional gifts that Paul mentions in Romans 12:3-8 **(Please read)**

What are the additional gifts that Paul mentions in Romans 12?

The Holy Spirit uses these gifts to glorify God and bless others through you. It is important that you are aware of the gifts God has given to you so that you know how He is at work through you. However, it is crucial that we do not become conceited in our gifts, rather give God all the glory for what is done.

Based on your list of strengths and weakness can you identify what gifts of the Spirit you may have been given?

Do not be disappointed if you cannot answer this question. Let it motivate you to seek after God and inquire of Him what gifts He has given to you!

God has created everyone uniquely with purpose and His gift of the Holy Spirit is at work through believers daily. Remember all gifts are empowered by the Holy Spirit to do God's work!

Please read:

Romans 12:3-8

Now let's go back to 1 Corinthians 12 and read verses 12-27.

What are Christians compared to in these two passages?

Why is it important to care for each other?

In marriage, how would you use this same analogy of a body comprised of parts compared to the relationship between a husband and wife?

Please read:

Genesis 2:24

Referring to 1 Corinthians 12:26 do you suffer when your husband suffers? Do you honor one another and rejoice together?

How can your spiritual gifts bless your husband?

Please read:

1 Corinthians 12:31
1 Corinthians 13

What is the greatest gift of the Spirit?

How can the gift of love radically impact your marriage?

Now let's look into the Fruit Of The Spirit:

What is the fruit of the Spirit?

Please read:

Galatians 5:22-26

What are the fruits of the Spirit listed in this passage?

Why do you think these characteristics are referred to as fruit?

Take a minute to write each fruit/characteristic, and then rate each one of these fruits according to your life.

0 = there is no evidence of that fruit being produced in your life

5 = there is a great amount of evidence of that fruit in your life

Do you have a few low ratings that need to be worked on?

Now take another minute to rate each fruit again, this time specifically according to the way you respond to your husband on a daily basis.

How do your numbers compare? What, if any, few low ratings do you need to work on in your marriage?

Which fruits are greatly evident in your husband's daily response towards you?

Galatians 5:25 encourages us to keep in step with the Spirit, how can you do this effectively?

How will an intentional increase in fruit production positively affect your relationship with God and your husband?

What changes can you make to produce an increase in fruit production?

Whether with gifts of the Spirit or fruits of the Spirit, remember: Don't imitate someone else's experiences. God desires a personal and unique relationship with you filled with personal and unique experiences!

Challenge:

Read 1 Corinthians 13:4-8 again and evaluate your life to see if there is an area of love that you can increase, especially in your marriage. For example, practicing having more patience or being kinder to your husband. Also, each day for the next week choose two fruits of the Spirit and intentionally increase productivity, specifically in your marriage.

*If you are up for an additional challenge, tell your husband you recognize that he is really good at (insert the gift or fruit of the Spirit your husband is good at blessing you with!) and thank him!! This will greatly affirm your husband.

This Week's Verses:

Romans 12
Galatians 5
1 Corinthians 13
John 15

Prayer Requests:

Take a few minutes to write down any prayer requests anyone may have and then lift them up in prayer.

SESSION 11:
INTENTIONAL INTIMACY

Did anyone experience any awesome breakthroughs this week or have praises to share?

Did anyone do the extra challenge from last week? If so, how did your husband respond?

Let's open this study with a prayer, asking the Holy Spirit to join us.

Dear Lord,

Thank you for each and every one of these ladies who have committed their time and devotion to participating in this group study. May you bless each of us, enrich our marriages, and continue to pour into our lives.

In Jesus name, amen.

Assignment #11 – Moments Of Intimacy

Take a few minutes to write down all the intimate moments you have shared with your husband in the last week. Remember, intimacy can be anything from sex to a special conversation to a romantic dinner.

Now spend about 1-2 minutes each giving a brief description of the current condition of your marriage out loud to the group, especially share any changes you have experienced since the beginning of this study. You do not have to share about what you just wrote down, but if you would like to add that you can.

Intentional Intimacy

Define Intimacy

There are many ways to define intimacy. Unfortunately, there is a connotation set in our society that intimacy is only sex. It is important for us to have a greater understanding of what intimacy is, and that while sex is an intimate experience that a husband and wife share, true intimacy is more than just sex. Intimacy is knowing someone deeply, being close to someone, and being familiar with someone. Intimacy requires vulnerability as those involved reveal very personal things encompassing the whole self, physically, spiritually, emotionally, and mentally.

God has designed us to be capable of being intimate. God designed marriage so that a husband and wife could experience an intimate love relationship, where they passionately pursue each other and love each other deeply. God created the marital union between a man and a woman to mirror His image and to reflect the intimate relationship between Jesus and His followers, both of which bring glory to God. Marriage is an opportunity to express unconditional, selfless, sacrificial love, just as Jesus did for us.

How can you intentionally grow closer to God?

In what ways do you think God pursues intimacy with you?

What does intimacy with God look like?

What keeps you from unveiling your whole self to God?

What does intimacy with your husband look like?

What keeps you from unveiling your whole self to your husband?

Please read:

Genesis 1:27

God designed people in His image and He desired to walk with His creation, intimately.

Please read:

Genesis 3:8-13

First acknowledge that God was walking in the garden, seeking man and his wife. God was pursuing an intimate love relationship with His creation. Yet, they were afraid and hid because they had sinned. Sin breaks fellowship with God and hinders intimacy.

Have you ever been afraid of God or hid from God because of sin in your life?

Have you ever been afraid, ashamed or have you ever hid from your husband because of sin?

How has sin affected your intimacy with God or with your husband?

When there is sin in our life we need to make sure that we confess and repent so that we may continue in an intimate relationship with God and our spouse.

Sin has made it impossible to be intimate with God; however, God sent His Son to be the atoning sacrifice so that we may be reconciled with God. So even after His creation sinned against Him, God still pursued an intimate love relationship with His people by sending His only Son to be the way to Him. Sin will hinder intimacy, but forgiveness restores it.

Have you ever experienced reconciliation with your husband through the power of forgiveness?

How does forgiveness cultivate intimacy in marriage?

Why is it important to forgive yourself in order to cultivate intimacy in relationships?

Just before Jesus was sacrificed He had a very intimate moment with His disciples.

Please read:

Matthew 26:20-30

Jesus had to be vulnerable in this moment with His disciples. He revealed things to them that were very personal, including who would betray Him and He also shared the symbolism of communion. Thousands of years later, the Church--the Bride of Christ--experiences intentional intimacy by participating in communion. Communion is remembering what Christ sacrificed to reconcile us to God, which is symbolized through breaking and eating bread and drinking wine/juice, representing Christ's body broken on the cross and His blood that was shed.

How can you experience intimacy with God during communion?

How can you experience intimacy with your husband during communion?

Just as Christ was vulnerable with His disciples, and revealed things to them, how can you be vulnerable with your husband and reveal things to him?

God so desperately pursues an intimate relationship with His people that even after Christ's resurrection, He sent the Holy Spirit as a comforter, to dwell inside believers.

Please read:

1 Corinthians 3:16-17
1 Corinthians 2:10-11

Your spirit knows you better and closer than anyone else. Likewise, God's Spirit knows Him better than anyone else. God desires to have such an intimate, personal relationship with you that He is willing to send His Spirit to live and dwell within you! It doesn't get any more personal than that! With the Holy Spirit inside of you, you and God experience oneness and He reveals things to you.

In what ways have you encountered intimacy with God?

What are some ways you can initiate intimacy with your husband?

Why is it important to cultivate intimacy in marriage?

What are some positive benefits of intimacy in marriage?

How has a lack of intimacy with your husband affected your marital relationship?

As was mentioned earlier, sex does not define intimacy; however, sex is an opportunity for a husband and wife to share one of the most intimate experiences of oneness.

Let's take a look at what scripture says about sexual intimacy in marriage.

Please read:

1 Corinthians 7:1-5

Why do you think Paul needed to encourage spouses not to deprive each other?

What things cause you to want to deprive your husband?

What kind of attitude should we have towards sex?

Just as we die to ourselves for the sake of Christ and the Church takes care of each other's needs, we should die to ourselves for the sake of our spouse and take care of his needs before our own. Whether towards God or your husband… having a positive and kind attitude, responding gently and respectfully, and meeting their needs before your own, will produce an intimate experience resulting in oneness in both relationships.

Challenge:

Intimacy is vital for marriage to thrive. Pursue at least one intimate experience with God and with your husband everyday.

This Week's Verses:

Psalm 63:1-8
Hebrews 13:4-6
Psalm 34:8-9
Ephesians 1:15-21

Reminder:

Everyone should bring a homemade dish/dessert next week!

Leader:

Be sure to bring everyone's letters written during session 1 to the next meeting.

Prayer Requests:

Take a few minutes to write down any prayer requests anyone may have and then lift them up in prayer.

Session 12:
The Great Commission

How was everyone's week?

Were you able to pursue God and your husband everyday?

Let us open this study with a prayer, inviting the Holy Spirit to move mightily.

Dear Lord,

Thank you again for this incredible time we had to build up relationships with each other while seeking after you! May you continue to inspire our hearts to chase after you daily. May we never lose hope and never lose faith. Holy Spirit, we surrender to you and ask that you would move mightily through us right now and forever.

In Jesus' name, amen.

Assignment #12 – Love Letter To God

Return each envelope back to the wives, which were collected during the first meeting.

Spend time reading your letter to yourself. On the opposite side of your letter to God, spend a few minutes replying to your letter from God's point of view, addressing everything you mentioned in your letter how you think God would respond to you.

Wait quietly for everyone to finish.

Does anyone feel led to share their letter?

Not everyone will want to, that is okay and it is okay if you only want to share parts of it. I will give you some time to consider sharing. **(If you, the leader, would like to go first, please do.)**

Now that everyone has had the opportunity to share let's talk about our experience with this assignment.

How did it make you feel to see where you were at to where you are now?

How did you feel writing from God's perspective?

What insights can you draw from writing from God's perspective? What does it reveal about what you know about God's truth?

In what ways has your marriage improved since the beginning of this study?

What personal changes have you experienced during this study?

<u>The Great Commission</u>

Define Disciple

The Great Commission mentioned by Jesus is found in Matthew 28:18-20. Read aloud.

Jesus gives us a call to action for believers to make disciples.

In what ways does Jesus explain how we can make disciples?

Jesus says that we can make disciples by sharing the truth of the gospel, baptizing, and teaching others.

This is a discipleship group, where I (the facilitator) had the opportunity to disciple all of you by leading you through God's Word, encouraging you and promoting accountability in your personal walk with God, as well as in your marriage.

Now you have the opportunity to disciple a group of wives. I implore each one of you to take your copy of this devotional and use it to lead another group of wives through this study.

I would now like to take a moment to share with you my testimony of leading this group study and then open it up for you to ask any questions you would have about leading a group like this.

Note From Unveiled Wife:

First of all, I would like to thank and honor your facilitator for having the courage to lead this group. You can applaud them along with me at this time!! Thank you for your dedication, your humility to serve, and your willingness to allow God to move through you in such a great way.

I also want to thank each wife so much for committing to being a part of this discipleship group and going through this devotional together. I hope that you have experienced God in a new way and have been encouraged in your relationship with Him and in your marriage with your husband. I believe that God pursued you to be here to grow and mature in Him, as well as purposefully to give you the opportunity to reach out and make more disciples. I believe that if you step out in faith, deciding to lead another group of wives through this group study, more women will experience growth in their relationships with God and marriages will be blessed. Please take your time to carefully consider this monumental opportunity to facilitate a wives group, praying and asking God to guide you in your decision. Thank you again for sharing in this journey to better your life and your marriage. May God bless you richly!

Challenge:

Pray about starting up another wives group just like the one you just finished. Pray about discipling other wives.

This Week's Verses:

Ephesians 4:11-16
Titus 2:1-8
Luke 6:40
Proverbs 27:17
John 15
1 Samuel 12:24
John 12:26
Romans 12:10-11
Galatians 5:13
1 Peter 4:10
Colossians 3:23-24

Prayer Requests:

Take a few minutes to pray for each one of your futures, including the condition and future of each marriage.

If this devotional has impacted your faith and marriage please let me know by posting a testimony here:
WivesAfterGod.com

For more marriage resources please visit:
unveiledwife.com/marriage-resources/

Recieve daily prayer for your marriage via email:
unveiledwife.com/daily-prayer/

Get connected:
Facebook.com/unveiledwife
Pinterest.com/unveiledwife
Youtube.com/unveiledwife
Instagram.com/unveiledwife
Twitter.com/unveiledwife

Get a copy of the 30-Day devotional
WifeAfterGod.com